FROM COMPUTE TO COMPETITIVENESS

Warrington Case Series

From Compute to Competitiveness

The Vice President for Research

MICHAEL CARRILLO

Warrington College of Business, University of Florida

Warrington Press / Gainesville

ACT I

THE SETUP

Pre-2020	2020	Jan 2021
CPU compute	$95M structure	HiPerGator AI

100 AI faculty commitment

A CPU-era research portfolio met a step change in compute capability and a faculty hiring commitment.

ACT II

THE OUTCOMES

4.56×
UF AI award growth
FY2017 ▯ FY2024

2.5–3.2×
outpacing of every national benchmark
Three convergent comparisons

20
UF colleges & affiliated centers
Cross-disciplinary diffusion

$511.8M
cumulative AI-classified awards in window
FY2021–FY2026YTD

INFRASTRUCTURE HiPerGator AI → **TALENT** Faculty + RSE → **AWARDS** 16 colleges + 4 centers

Hardware enabled talent; talent enabled awards. The mechanism was indirect—and the data shows the lag.

ACT III

THE RECKONING

What can a VP for Research credibly claim?

Three tiers: will claim, claim with caveats, will not claim.

A protagonist who distinguishes what the evidence supports from what it merely tempts them to say.

I. THE QUESTION

On the second floor of the McKnight Brain Institute, computational neuroscientists were using deep learning models to distinguish Parkinsonian disorders using imaging data alone. A floor below, kidney pathologists were training computational image-analysis platforms with a federal atlas of human biomolecular tissue. Across campus, a College of Education researcher was building an adaptive learning system that had already enrolled tens of thousands of K–12 students. In a College of Engineering lab, a team sponsored by the Defense Advanced Research Projects Agency (DARPA) was developing AI-driven task guidance for soldiers operating in extreme conditions.

The projects appeared to have little in common. They were housed in different colleges, served different federal sponsors, and applied AI to distinct problems. What unified them was compute. Each depended, directly or indirectly, on the same university-owned supercomputer.

The University of Florida deployed HiPerGator AI in January 2021. By 2026, AI-related federal awards at UF had grown more than fourfold and spanned twenty colleges and affiliated centers. The growth extended into sponsor ecosystems where UF had little visible AI presence five years earlier: education, health, national security, energy, and defense. The US Department of Education, the National Institutes of Health's (NIH) Human BioMolecular Atlas Program (HuBMAP) consortium, the Department of Energy's National Nuclear Security Administration, and DARPA were now part of UF's AI research story.

The portfolio was still taking shape. New organizational structures, including the Digital Brain Initiative, the Intensive Care Unit of Tomorrow, and the Artificial Intelligence and Informatics Research Institute, were positioning UF to compete for grants the federal government had not yet announced.

For David Norton, UF's Vice President for Research, the numbers were encouraging yet incomplete.

The question he knew was coming was the obvious one: How much of this growth would have occurred anyway? It could come from a board member, a peer vice president for research, a conference audience member, or a dean. Norton understood why it was fair to ask. Use of AI had surged across science in the same years, drawing new federal funding and pulling researchers in nearly every field toward computational methods; some of UF's growth was almost certainly part of that larger movement. But a national wave does not staff a laboratory or write a proposal. The number of researchers doing intensive computational work did not change simply because UF bought a computer. In the beginning, the university had to create demand on the research side.

Now Norton had to explain what had changed, why it mattered, and how much HiPerGator AI had shifted UF's research trajectory.

II. THE SETUP

In 2019, the University of Florida was a public university with a research portfolio approaching $900 million. Its position in federal research and development rankings was respectable, though outside the top twenty-five. Its high-performance computing platform, the original HiPerGator cluster, had been built for traditional scientific workloads: fluid dynamics, climate modeling, computational chemistry, and other central processing unit (CPU)–intensive applications. AI workloads were possible at UF, but they were not the platform's strength. The emerging generation of deep learning research required the kind of parallel matrix arithmetic that graphics processing units (GPUs) made tractable.

What changed in 2020 was not simply the size of the investment. It was the structure of the deal. Chris Malachowsky, a UF alumnus and cofounder of NVIDIA, made a $30 million personal gift. NVIDIA matched it with $30 million in hardware and technical support. UF committed $15 million to upgrade its data center infrastructure to host the new system. These three non-recurring commitments were joined by $20 million in recurring annual funding from the State of Florida to support the hiring of more than one hundred AI-focused faculty members across sixteen colleges.

The result was a partnership rather than a single grant. Each party addressed a different constraint: hardware, facilities, technical support, faculty capacity, operations, and recurring institutional commitment. The architecture was deliberate. UF was acquiring more than an AI supercomputer; it was attempting to build the institutional system around it.

Although the deal's architecture would later prove decisive for the research enterprise, the original institutional commitment was not framed in research terms. When Malachowsky first asked Provost Joe Glover what UF would do with an AI supercomputer, Glover's answer was educational. UF would teach AI across the curriculum, rather than confining it to computer science or engineering, and would make it accessible to any student willing to engage with it.

That commitment, made in January 2020 before a research thesis had been fully articulated, became the AI initiative's organizing principle. The grant-competitiveness story that anchors this case was a derivative thesis, developed inside the Office of the Vice President for Research (VPR) as the implications of the gift became clear. It rested on the assumption that an educational commitment of this scale would attract faculty, build capability, and create the institutional conditions that competitive research would later require.

UF did not initially justify the supercomputer primarily as a research growth investment. Instead, it justified the investment as a means of teaching AI to all students. The research portfolio that followed was, in part, a second-order consequence of that educational decision.

HiPerGator AI became operational in January 2021. The system comprised 140 NVIDIA DGX A100 nodes and consumed more than a megawatt of power. On paper, it represented a step change in capability. UF had moved from CPU-dominant scientific computing to GPU-dense AI computing in a single deployment.

Norton, who had been Vice President for Research for nearly two decades, understood the distinction between technical capacity and research productivity. The machine itself was only one investment, he would later explain. UF would also need people who could stand between faculty researchers and the machine: research computing staff, AI specialists, facilitators, and technical translators who could help scholars turn disciplinary questions into computational workflows. The university needed to figure out that layer quickly and begin hiring before demand fully materialized.

The investment thesis, articulated in pre-deployment briefings and the original AI initiative documents, made four specific predictions. First, AI infrastructure would become a differentiator in faculty recruiting. Second, it would enable UF to compete for center-scale federal awards requiring dedicated computational resources. Third, it would broaden AI research beyond engineering and computing into the health

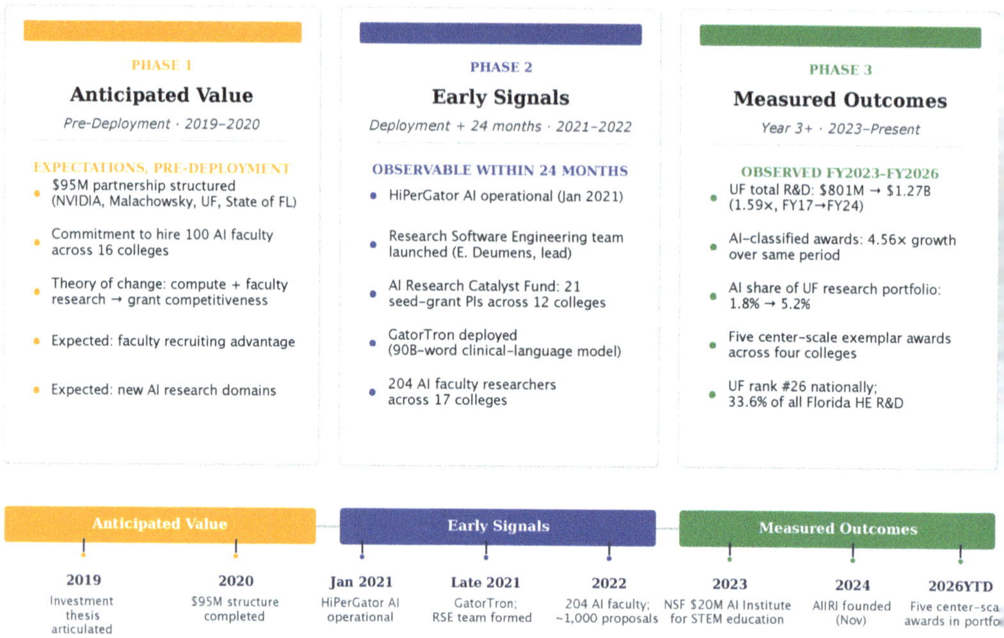

EXHIBIT 1. Research Value Realization Timeline

sciences, agriculture, education, and the social sciences. Finally, it would generate measurable growth in federally funded AI research over a five-year horizon (Exhibit 1).

Those were the expectations. The harder question was whether the institutional system could turn computational capacity into outcomes.

III. THE LAG AND THE LESSON

HiPerGator AI became operational in January 2021, yet the visible inflection in UF's AI award curve did not appear until FY22. For roughly eighteen months, the indicator at the center of this case remained essentially flat. The machine was available, but the institutional capability to translate compute capacity into funded AI research was still forming (Exhibit 2).

Norton's reading of that period was unsentimental. The number of people doing intensive computational work did not increase simply

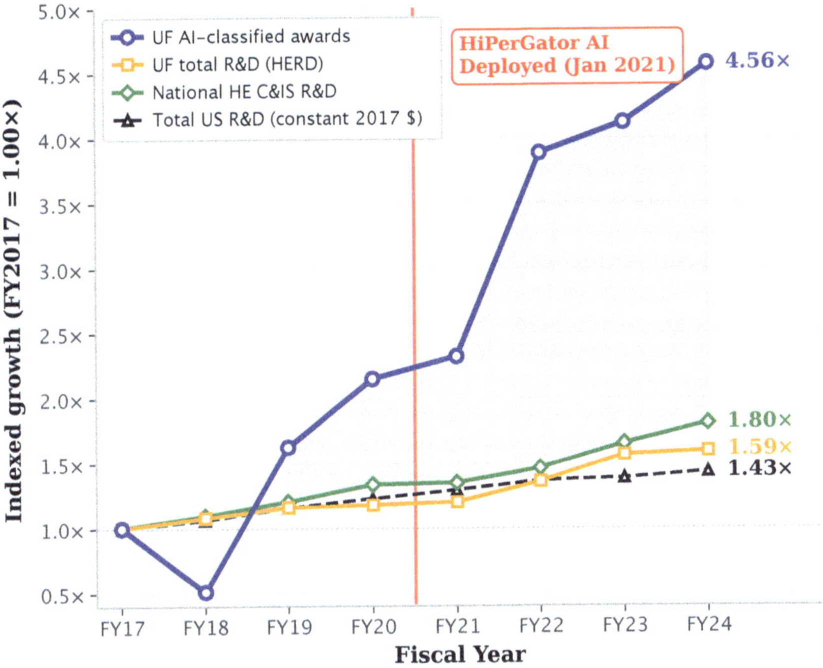

FY2017 → FY2024 GROWTH RATIOS

UF AI awards grew **4.56×** *between FY2017 and FY2024*

2.87×	**2.53×**	**3.19×**
vs. UF total R&D	**vs. National HE C&IS**	**vs. Total US R&D**
Scenario A	*Scenario B*	*Scenario C*

UF AI growth outpaced every benchmark by 2.5-3.2×.

Convergence across three independent benchmarks suggests a UF-specific effect.

EXHIBIT 2. Indexed Growth Comparison: UF AI Awards vs. National Benchmarks

because UF bought the computer. In many ways, the university was constrained by the computational talent already present among the faculty.

The expectation in 2020 had been more linear: Capacity would arrive, researchers would use it, proposals would follow, and awards would land. The reality was less direct. A 140-node DGX A100 cluster did not, by itself, create faculty who knew how to write competitive AI proposals to the National Science Foundation (NSF), NIH, Department of Energy, or DARPA. It did not give a kidney pathologist or an education researcher a graduate student capable of moving a job through a Slurm queue. It did not produce the pilot data needed to distinguish a fundable AI proposal from a speculative one.

The machine could enable those outcomes only when people were prepared to use it. In 2021, across a research portfolio spanning sixteen colleges, readiness was uneven. For a time, HiPerGator AI represented latent institutional capacity: powerful infrastructure awaiting the faculty expertise, research workflows, and organizational routines needed to activate it.

The mechanism that began to close the gap was not primarily faculty recruiting, though hiring continued. It was the Artificial Intelligence Research Catalyst Fund: twenty $50,000 proof-of-concept awards made by Norton's office in December 2020, one month before HiPerGator AI went live. The awards were deliberately distributed across colleges to seed AI-enabled research in fields where AI had not previously been central.

Norton described the Catalyst Fund as supporting six- to eight-month studies that enabled small research teams to engage immediately with the new computational capability. Many projects paired disciplinary faculty with engineering or AI specialists to translate research questions into computational workflows. The grants funded a student assistant or postdoc, covered the cost of an initial run on the new machine, and produced the figures, preliminary results, and methods sections that federal AI proposals often required.

From the operations side, Erik Deumens, research computing director under Chief Information Officer Elias Eldayrie, viewed the same mechanism differently. The seed program was not primarily about recruiting new investigators to UF. It helped investigators already at UF convert AI ideas into competitive proposals. The funding gave them credibility, pilot results, and enough methodological footing to pursue external grants. In many cases, they won those grants.

From Deumens's vantage point, demand for the system did not increase on the deployment date. It climbed in 2021, rose further in 2022, and accelerated in 2023. That period also marked the start of UF's divergence from the comparative benchmarks in Exhibit 2.

That sequence—seed funding to pilot results to proposals to awards—was the indirect mechanism the case was built to surface. Hardware enabled work; it did not perform work. HiPerGator AI produced little measurable change in award volume during its first eighteen months because compute was not the only binding constraint. UF also needed researchers prepared to frame AI questions, technical staff able to support them, pilot data and experience strong enough to anchor proposals, and time for federal review cycles to run.

The lag, then, was not evidence against the investment thesis. It revealed the thesis. The seed program, central support model, faculty hiring effort, and four-party deal structure were all designed to close the gap between installed capacity and research output.

Norton's framing was straightforward. Seed money mattered because it gave people a place to start. That work led to proposals, which in turn led to grants. The image UF's infrastructure planners had used—a race car without a pit crew—applied to research computing operations and to faculty research capacity alike: The machine could not win races without people to run it. The FY21–FY22 inflection in Exhibit 2 showed what it looked like when the crew began to arrive.

IV. THE MEASURABLE AND THE UNMEASURABLE

By FY26, the numbers were difficult to dismiss. UF AI-classified federal awards had grown 4.56 times over the FY17 baseline, the steepest increase among the four series shown in Exhibit 2. Over the same period, UF's total R&D expenditures grew 1.59 times, national higher education R&D in computer and information sciences grew 1.80 times, and total US R&D, measured in constant 2017 dollars, grew 1.43 times.

The resulting ratios converged. UF AI awards outpaced UF total R&D by 2.87 times, national computer and information sciences R&D by 2.53

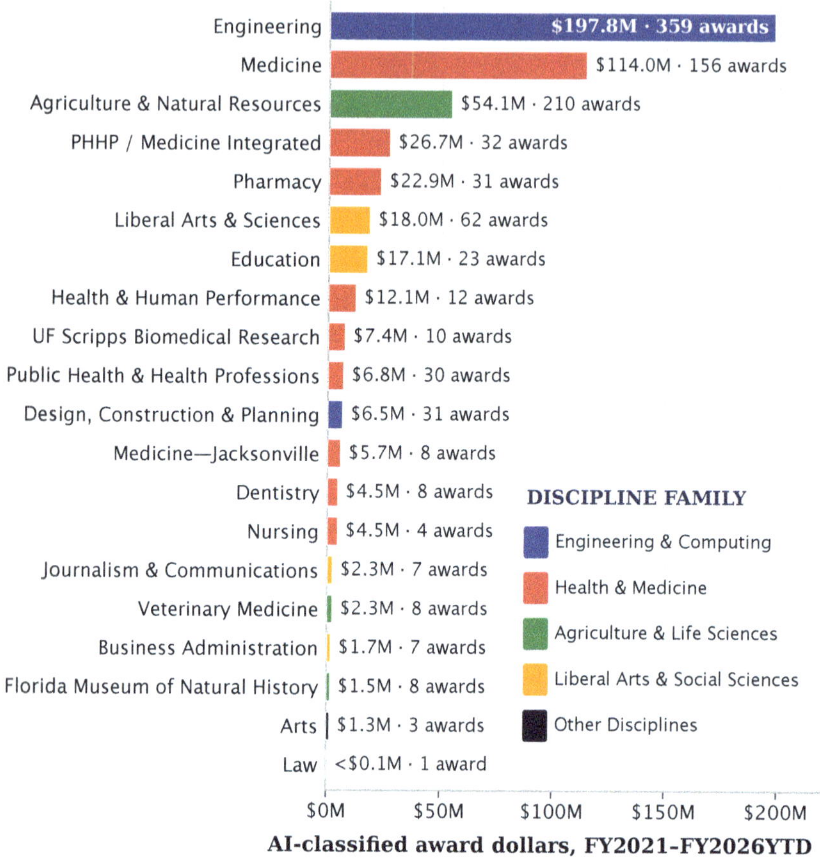

PORTFOLIO TOTALS

20
UF colleges & affiliated centers

$511.8M
total AI-classified awards, FY21–FY26YTD

1,024
individual AI-classified awards in this window

All-AI series (see Appendix A)

EXHIBIT 3. AI Award Breadth by College

times, and total US R&D by 3.19 times. Taken together, the comparisons suggested that UF's AI research growth was roughly 2.5 to 3.2 times larger than a set of reasonable national and institutional benchmarks.

The breadth of the portfolio also changed. Between FY21 and FY26 year-to-date, AI-classified awards reached twenty UF colleges and affiliated centers, totaling $511.8 million across 1,024 awards (Exhibit 3). UF's National Science Foundation Higher Education Research and Development (HERD) rank climbed to number twenty-six nationally, and 33.6 percent of all higher education R&D in Florida occurred at UF.

The next question, the one Norton had been preparing for, was how anyone could know. Before the growth could be attributed, it had to be measured.

For most of the period covered by Exhibit 2, UF could not know with precision. Like many research portfolios, its AI portfolio had been tracked through keyword searches of proposal titles and abstracts, using an evolving list of terms. Alina Zare, director of UF's Artificial Intelligence and Informatics Research Institute (AIIRI), described the limitation directly: Keyword searches could capture some awards and miss others. An award titled "Adaptive Learning Systems for K–12 Mathematics" might or might not be tagged as AI, depending on the analyst, the timing of the search, and the keyword list in use. The same award, classified twice, could fall on opposite sides of the line. There was no systematic way to know what the search process had missed.

That imprecision became evident in September 2025, when the UF Board of Trustees (BOT) received an AI award summary based on a manual-search methodology. It reported approximately $230 million year-to-date for FY21 through FY26. Eight months later, the dataset anchoring this case reported $342.5 million in High-confidence AI awards for the same period, roughly 50 percent higher.

The difference was not a correction. Both numbers reflected the answers the available method could produce at the time the question was asked.

Over the intervening eight months, the key change was the introduction of a tool. The AIIRI built IntelliGator: a large language model–based award classifier that scanned roughly 22,000 award records and rated each one for AI relevance using a four-tier rubric. The tool ran on-premises so that future iterations could process confidential data covered by UF's existing compliance certifications. Appendix A describes the classifier, the rubric, and the corpus in detail.

What mattered for the figures in this case was the design philosophy. IntelliGator was built as a strict, high-precision classifier, instructed to default to lower confidence tiers when uncertain. As a result, it was more likely to miss AI-relevant awards than to include weakly related ones. Awards whose metadata lacked explicit AI language were systematically excluded, even when the underlying research was AI-driven. A recent National Nuclear Security Administration (NNSA) award supporting UF's role in the Department of Energy's Predictive Science Academic Alliance Program (PSAAP), for example, was not flagged because the underlying database record did not reference AI methods. The $342.5 million High-confidence figure and the broader $511.8 million All-AI figure were therefore conservative lower-bound estimates.

Yet IntelliGator's errors differed from those of human searchers using evolving keyword lists. They were systematic. Each award was classified consistently using the same model, rubric, and prompt. Inter-rater variance—the disagreement or inconsistency among human reviewers—was replaced by a single, consistent, auditable bias.

This case was therefore based on the second dataset, not the first. That choice created a recursive observation that was more than a rhetorical flourish: UF used AI to evaluate the impact of its investment in AI infrastructure. The same hardware purchased to enable AI research at scale also ran the classifier that quantified how much AI research the investment helped produce. The case's headline numbers were, in a literal operational sense, generated by the system whose value they described.

One further correction belonged here. UF's compliance certifications, including HITRUST, NIST 800-171, and the Cybersecurity Maturity Model Certification (CMMC) pathway, were sometimes folded into the AI infrastructure story because they were visible features of the post-deployment environment. Norton had been clear that they were, in fact, complementary investments into the university's research computing enterprise. The FISMA-grade secure environment had been established in 2015 to support a $40 million federal grant, and the HITRUST pursuit began before the NVIDIA partnership was announced. The AI investment inherited that posture; it did not create it. Section V returns to this distinction. However, without the above-referenced certifications and related secure environments, opportunities within the AI area would be missed.

Exhibit 4 shows what the dataset captured at the project level: five High-confidence awards, four colleges, five funders, and $23.3 million in total. Leite's $8.9 million Virtual Learning Lab in the College of Education, funded by the US Department of Education's Institute of Education Sciences, was the largest of the five. Sarder's NIH-funded HuBMAP-aligned computational pathology platform in the College of Medicine totaled $4.9 million. Vaillancourt's NIH National Institute of Neurological Disorders and Stroke–funded web-based imaging differentiation system for Parkinsonism, housed in the College of Health and Human Performance, also totaled $4.9 million. Ruiz's DARPA-funded ENKIx (Enabling Knowledgeable Task Guidance in the Extremes) project in the College of Engineering totaled $4.0 million. The exhibit records one further award outside the dataset: Balachandar's $10.15 million PSAAP award, supported through Triad National Security and obligated in May 2026 after the dataset's cut date, sourced from Sponsored Programs records rather than IntelliGator—a project-level instance of the classifier conservatism described above.

V. THE RECKONING

If a peer institution's vice president for research had called Norton in mid-2026 and asked, "Was it worth it?" Norton's answer would not have been a number. It would have been a structure—and an opportunity.

The structure had three tiers, and Norton had carefully considered which claims belonged in each. In his April 2026 interview, when asked what he would say to a skeptical provost about the research return on HiPerGator AI, what he would claim, and what he would explicitly avoid claiming, he began with the educational case.

It started, he said, with better preparing students for forty-five years in the workplace. Both undergraduate and graduate students needed exposure to the tools and methods they would encounter after graduation. For UF graduates, AI would be a major part of that environment. Developing curricula and opportunities across disciplines would give

Award	PI	Funder	Period	Amount	College	Why it matters
Center of Excellence: Assured Autonomy in Contested Environments	Warren Dixon	US Air Force AFOSR	2019–2027	**$8.19M**	Engineering	*Air Force Center of Excellence in autonomy under contested conditions. Prestige-tier federal AI investment.*
Precision Education: The Virtual Learning Lab	Walter Leite	US Dept of Education IES	2016–2022	**$8.9M**	Education	*AI-driven adaptive learning at scale. Demonstrates pre-2021 AI capability accelerated by HiPerGator.*
Computational Image Analysis Platform (CIMAP) for HuBMAP	Pinaki Sarder	NIH (Office of the Director) HuBMAP Consortium	2022–2026	**$4.9M**	Medicine	*Multi-modal image AI for human biomolecular atlas. Anchor for sustained NIH AI-imaging program at UF.*
Web-Based Automated Imaging Differentiation of Parkinsonism	David Vaillancourt	NIH / NINDS	2021–2027	**$4.9M**	Health & Human Performance	*Deep-learning diagnostic imaging beyond Engineering/Medicine core. Cross-college AI penetration evidence.*
ENKIx: Enabling Knowledgeable Task Guidance In the Extremes	Jaime Ruiz	DARPA US Dept of Defense	2021–2024	**$4.0M**	Engineering	*AI for high-stakes operational task guidance. DARPA-funded—the federal AI defense-research tier.*
External to IntelliGator Dataset						*Source: UF [Division of Sponsored Programs]*
Predictive Science Academic Alliance Program (PSAAP) Multi-Phase Flow Physics	S. "Bala" Balachandar	DOE / NNSA via Triad National Security	2025–2030	**$10.15M**	Engineering	*Exascale AI/ML for multiphase flow. Norton (interview, Apr 2026): "HiPerGator was key" to PSAAP win.*

EXHIBIT 4. Exemplar AI Awards at the University of Florida

students experience and competency with AI, making them more effective at presenting their skills and competing in the labor market.

He then moved to the research side, and the language shifted from preparation to capacity. An institutional AI capability mattered. Some work could be done in the cloud and billed as needed. But certain "hero projects" required reserving a significant share of a dedicated system for complex AI computations. To compete for that class of work, Norton believed a university needed its own machine.

Finally, he turned to faculty recruiting, where he framed the argument as conditional on institutional ambition. Institutions that did not aspire to be among the most competitive R1 universities might not need such a capability, but those seeking to compete for top faculty in AI-enabled fields did. For UF, he argued, the payoff had been substantial. Lacking that capability over the next five years would put a university at a disadvantage.

These were the claims Norton would make without qualification. They shared a structural property worth noting: None were primarily about award dollars. They also included claims about capability—what UF could do, who UF could hire, and what UF could offer its students. Capability could be assessed directly, without requiring a counterfactual model of federal funding flows. This is the first tier of Exhibit 5: the tier where Norton did not need to prove what would have happened otherwise.

The second tier was where the counterfactual mattered and where Norton was willing to argue with caveats. UF's 4.56× growth in AI awards, the spread of those awards across twenty colleges and centers, and the convergent benchmark ratios in Exhibit 2 were real and measurable. But they occurred during a period of surging national AI funding, proliferating federal AI program codes, and a broad shift in the academic research ecosystem toward computational methods.

Norton's own framing was careful. When an investment in computational resources accounted for a large share of sponsored research activity, determining which projects were specifically enabled by that investment and which would have happened anyway was difficult. The case's position, and Norton's, is that the convergence of the three benchmark ratios is hard to explain without an institutional effect. UF AI growth outpaced UF total R&D by 2.87×, national computer and information sciences R&D by 2.53×, and total US R&D by 3.19×. Three

EXHIBIT 5. Norton's Claim Spectrum: Three Tiers of Defensible Attribution

different reference points all pointing in the same direction is not what coincidence usually looks like.

But "hard to explain without" is not proof. The signal was consistent with the investment, but it was not exclusively caused by it. The national surge was real and of comparable magnitude. Federal nondefense AI R&D investment roughly doubled between FY2021 and FY2025—the same window over which UF's AI awards also roughly doubled. However, UF's AI awards had already more than doubled between FY2017 and FY2021, ahead of the federal AI funding ramp—a pattern more consistent with an institution that built capacity early than with one that simply rose with the tide. Tier two was where Norton could defend the claim while acknowledging that he could not fully rule out alternative explanations.

The third tier was where Norton refused to make claims at all. He initially downplayed the compliance attribution. UF's HITRUST certification, NIST 800-171 environment, and CMMC pathway were sometimes folded into the AI infrastructure narrative because they were visible features of the post-deployment institution. But those capabilities predated the AI investment. The FISMA-grade environment had been built in 2015 for an earlier federal grant, and the HITRUST pursuit had begun before the NVIDIA partnership was announced. HiPerGator AI inherited a compliance posture rather than creating one. Yet this combination provided unique competitive research opportunities.

Second, he rejected the clean UF-versus-national counterfactual. The measurement infrastructure described in Section IV could quantify the composition of UF's AI award portfolio, but it could not quantify what the portfolio would have looked like in a parallel universe in which the Malachowsky gift had never occurred. No method could fully quantify that.

Third, he was cautious regarding the portfolio-shift causation argument that some institutions might have been tempted to make. When asked whether AI infrastructure had changed the composition of UF's research portfolio—toward larger awards, multi-PI collaborations, and cross-college work—Norton was unwilling to credit the machine with the shift. The research questions UF was paid to investigate, including crop pathogens, medical imaging, learning systems, and fluid mechanics, predated HiPerGator AI and would persist after it. What changed was the toolkit.

The three tiers—what Norton would claim, what he would claim with caveats, and what he would not claim—are the most useful part of the case for readers evaluating institutional AI investments elsewhere (Exhibit 5). Most return-on-investment arguments at this scale collapse these tiers into a single category, treating capability, growth, and counterfactual claims as if they share the same evidentiary status. They do not.

Norton's discipline about which claims rested on which kind of evidence was, in the end, the most transferable lesson the UF experience offered. The machine was one thing. The argument for the machine was another. They were not the same, and they should not have been defended the same way.

What a vice president for research could credibly claim about a $95 million AI infrastructure investment depended on the type of claim being made, the evidence available to support it, and whether the institution had built the measurement infrastructure to know the difference.

By mid-2026, UF had built that infrastructure. The question was no longer whether HiPerGator AI had changed the university, but which changes UF could prove, which it could reasonably argue, and which it had the discipline to leave unclaimed.

The question Norton had been preparing for—How much of this growth would have occurred anyway?—did not have a clean answer, and Norton had stopped looking for one. No measurement system, however well designed, could reconstruct the parallel universe in which the Malachowsky gift had never occurred. The convergence of three benchmark ratios was the strongest signal the available evidence could produce, and it was not proof. What, in the end, separated a credible research leader from a merely enthusiastic one was the willingness to say so.

APPENDIX A: DATA SOURCES AND CLASSIFICATION METHODOLOGY

The empirical backbone of this case is a dataset of 1,582 sponsored research awards at the University of Florida, classified as AI-related by IntelliGator, a large-language-model classifier developed by the Artificial Intelligence and Informatics Research Institute under the direction of Alina Zare in collaboration with research software engineers. IntelliGator is built on Llama 3.3 70B Instruct and runs natively on UF AI Navi-

Gator, hosted on HiPerGator. The classifier evaluates three fields from each award record: title, description, and keywords. The description and keywords fields vary widely across award records, ranging from a few words to long narratives. Applied to a corpus of roughly 22,000 sponsored research award records, it uses a four-tier rubric embedded in the system prompt to identify awards with a substantive relationship to artificial intelligence.

The Classification Rubric

The rubric distinguishes four levels of AI relevance. **High** classifications require explicit reference to artificial intelligence, machine learning, or closely related AI terminology in the award metadata. **Medium** classifications capture awards that describe prototypical AI tasks, such as image classification, object detection, machine translation, speech recognition, document classification, prediction, or similar forms of computational inference, even when the metadata does not explicitly name an AI or machine learning approach. **Low** classifications apply when AI is mentioned but not substantively used, such as a project that teaches about AI without applying AI methods. **None** applies when the award metadata contains no AI- or machine learning–related terms.

For the purposes of this case, the dataset retains only awards classified as **High** or **Medium**. Awards classified as **Low** or **None** were excluded upstream because they did not represent substantive AI-related research activity.

A Strict High-Precision Design

IntelliGator's system prompt frames the tool as "a strict high-precision classifier" and instructs the model to "default to Low or None when unsure." This design choice favors precision over recall, creating an important methodological consequence: Awards whose metadata lacks AI-specific language are systematically excluded, even when the underlying research may be AI-driven.

The PSAAP example discussed in Section IV illustrates this pattern. The NNSA-funded grant supporting UF's role in the Department of Energy's Predictive Science Academic Alliance Program was not flagged by IntelliGator because the award database record did not reference

AI methods. As a result, the figures reported in this case should be interpreted as conservative lower-bound estimates of UF's AI-related sponsored research activity, rather than upper-bound estimates.

Why Both High and Medium Tiers Are Reported

This case examines whether institutional investment in computing infrastructure generated downstream research outcomes. For that question, both **High** and **Medium** classifications should be included in the analysis. A predictive crop-disease model trained on HiPerGator draws on the same compute investment as an award titled "Artificial Intelligence for Orthodontic Prediction," regardless of whether the term "AI" appears explicitly in the abstract.

Excluding **Medium** awards would understate the institutional return by ignoring cases in which AI serves as a research methodology rather than the named object of study. In those projects, AI may not be the headline topic, but it still drives the scientific work.

For that reason, the case reports two series throughout. The **High-confidence series** is the headline measure: $342.5 million in cumulative funding across FY21–FY26 YTD, representing 640 awards in which AI is explicitly named in the award metadata. The broader **All-AI series**, which combines **High** and **Medium** classifications, totals $511.8 million in cumulative funding across 1,024 awards over the same window; the full classified corpus underlying the case comprises 1,582 awards across all fiscal years. This second series captures the wider body of AI-dependent research activity at UF.

A Note on the Rising High-Confidence Share over Time

One feature of the data warrants explicit acknowledgment. The share of AI-classified awards assigned to the **High-confidence** tier rose from roughly 25 percent in FY17 to 71 percent in FY26. Two non-exclusive forces likely explain this shift.

The first is a substantive shift in UF's research portfolio. As AI matured and UF's institutional investments expanded through HiPerGator, AIIRI, and the AI Across the Curriculum initiative, AI moved from an enabling methodology to a named research focus. The second is a change in the language of grantsmanship. In the post-2022 environment, investigators increasingly name AI explicitly in proposals, whereas earlier versions of similar work may have foregrounded the application domain rather than the underlying computational method.

This distinction matters for interpreting the growth figures. From FY17 to FY24, the **High-confidence** series increased 4.56×, while the broader **All-AI** series increased 2.00×. Both figures are accurate, but they answer different questions. The 4.56× figure captures the growing visibility of AI within UF's research identity. The 2.00× figure captures the underlying growth in AI-dependent and compute-enabled research activity. The case uses both measures, with attention to the question each one is designed to answer.

A Note on Time Windows

Two analytical windows appear in the case, each serving a distinct purpose. Cumulative dollar figures use the **FY21–FY26 YTD** window to focus on the post-HiPerGator AI investment period. This period is most relevant to the case's central question: whether UF's compute investment translated into downstream sponsored research activity.

Growth-rate comparisons use **FY17–FY24**, the longest complete-year window spanning both the pre- and post-investment eras. This window allows the trajectory of AI-related research activity to be observed before, during, and after the visible inflection point.

Known Limitations

Three limitations of the IntelliGator approach are important for readers evaluating the methodology. First, the classifier examines only three metadata fields: title, description, and keywords. It does not analyze the full proposal text. As a result, awards whose full abstracts or technical narratives clearly involve AI may be misclassified or missed entirely if that relationship is not evident in the award metadata.

Second, as discussed above, IntelliGator's strict, high-precision design produces conservative figures. The classifier is intentionally more likely to exclude ambiguous awards than to include awards with weak evidence of AI relevance.

Third, the dataset does not directly measure HiPerGator utilization. AI classification serves as a proxy for compute-dependent research, but it is imperfect. It omits computationally intensive non-AI workloads, such as molecular dynamics, climate modeling, and high-energy physics simulations, that also use UF's institutional compute infrastructure. It may also include AI-related work conducted on non-UF infrastructure.

A future iteration of this analysis could cross-reference AI-classified awards with HiPerGator allocation and utilization records. That step would yield a tighter measure of the relationship among AI infrastructure, researcher adoption, and sponsored research outcomes.

Data Access and Reproducibility

The underlying award list, IntelliGator classification labels, classifier system prompt, and aggregation workbook used to produce the case exhibits are available on request from the UF Artificial Intelligence and Informatics Research Institute, UF Research Computing, or the case author. Researchers seeking to replicate or extend the classification approach should contact AIIRI directly for information about the IntelliGator pipeline.

APPENDIX B: SOURCES CONSULTED

The empirical and interpretive content of this case draws on the sources listed below. All interviews were conducted in person. Internal University of Florida documents were provided by the designated offices. Federal statistical sources are publicly available through the National Center for Science and Engineering Statistics (NCSES) and the National Science Board.

Interviews

The five interviews listed below were conducted as part of the broader four-micro-case series that accompanies the macro case *Building an AI University* (Carrillo 2026). Interview-based research for this case received an exempt determination from the University of Florida Institutional Review Board (Protocol ET00053389, approved April 27, 2026). Only the Norton interview and the Zare-Gray meeting directly address the empirical content of this Vice President for Research micro case; the others are cited for context within the series.

Eldayrie, Elias, and Erik Deumens. 2026. Interview by Michael Carrillo. UF Chief Information Officer (Eldayrie); Director, UF

Research Computing (Deumens). May 12. Gainesville, FL. Subject: technical deployment of HiPerGator AI, the Research Software Engineering team, and the post-deployment support model referenced in Section III. Cited for series context; details forthcoming in the Chief Information Officer micro case.

Glover, Joseph. 2026. Interview by Michael Carrillo. UF Provost and Senior Vice President for Academic Affairs. May 15. Gainesville, FL. Subject: institutional governance of the AI initiative, the AI Across the Curriculum framework, and the role of the AI2 Center. Cited for series context; details forthcoming in the Provost micro case.

Martin, Maria, and Jessica Storm Steele. 2026. Interview by Michael Carrillo. UF Vice President for Advancement (Martin); UF Advancement (Steele). May 4. Gainesville, FL. Subject: philanthropic strategy and donor-relations dimensions of the Malachowsky partnership. Cited for series context; details forthcoming in the Vice President for Advancement micro case.

Norton, David. 2026. Interview by Michael Carrillo. UF Vice President for Research. April 28. Gainesville, FL. Subject: HiPerGator AI investment, AI Research Catalyst Fund, research portfolio growth, attribution methodology, and the three-tier claim framework discussed in Section V.

Zare, Alina, and Stephanie Gray. 2026. Joint meeting with Michael Carrillo. Director, UF Artificial Intelligence and Informatics Research Institute (Zare); UF Associate Vice President, Division of Sponsored Programs (Gray). May 14. Gainesville, FL. Subject: IntelliGator classification methodology, NCSES benchmarking guidance, NSF/NIH grant accounting differences, and the methodological reconciliation between the September 2025 BOT figure and the IntelliGator-derived totals reported in Section IV.

Internal University of Florida Documents

Carrillo, Michael. 2026. *Building an AI University*. Warrington Press. [Companion macro case providing institutional context for the four micro cases, including this Vice President for Research micro case.]

Glover, Joseph, and David Norton. 2021. *The University of Florida Initiative in Artificial Intelligence and Data Science*. January. UF Office of the Provost and Office of the Vice President for Research. [Foundational document describing HiPerGator AI deployment, the four-party partnership structure, and the AI Across the Curriculum framework as articulated at the time of system launch.]

Glover, Joseph, and David Norton. 2023. "UF AI Update: Building an AI University." March. Presentation to the UF Board of Trustees. [Status report on the UF AI initiative's progress two years post-deployment, including faculty hiring, partnerships, curricular reach, and research activity. Documents over 230 AI and data science courses across colleges and over 300 AI faculty members.]

Norton, David. 2022. *AI Research Activity FY2022*. UF Office of the Vice President for Research. [Internal infographic reporting 204 active AI/Data Science researchers, $13 million in new AI/Data Science awards received in FY2022, $141 million in funding proposals under review, and 156 AI/Data Science proposals submitted. Source for the faculty headcount and proposal-volume figures cited in Exhibit 1, Phase 2.]

Norton, David. 2022. "UF AI Research Update." UF Office of the Vice President for Research. [Internal presentation reporting approximately 1,000 AI-related research proposals submitted since the initiative began, totaling over $800 million in proposal budgets and approximately $70 million in awards to date. Source for figures in Exhibit 1, Phase 2.]

Norton, David. 2025. "AI Research at UF: Board of Trustees Briefing." September. UF Board of Trustees. [BOT presentation reporting approximately $230 million in AI-related awards FY21–FY26 YTD, using the manual-keyword classification methodology that predates IntelliGator. Discussed in Section IV in the context of methodological reconciliation.]

UF Office of the Vice President for Research. 2020. *AI Catalyst Awardee Synopses*. December 7. [Internal compilation of the twenty $50,000 proof-of-concept awards distributed by the VPR office one month before HiPerGator AI went operational. Documents seed-grant recipients across twelve colleges and serves as the source for the AI Research Catalyst Fund references in Section III and Exhibit 1.]

UF Office of the Vice President for Research. 2025. *VPR AI Awards Analysis, version 4*. Master analytical workbook. [Primary empirical source for this case. Includes the IntelliGator-classified award

records (1,582 awards, all fiscal years), embedded NCSES HERD source tables, NCSES National Patterns Table 1, the three National Benchmark scenarios, the breakdown of awards by college and sponsor, and the exhibit aggregations underlying Exhibits 2, 3, and 5.]
Zare, Alina, and Ron Fick. 2026. "UFR IntelliGator Demo." UF AI Research Senior Executive Meeting, May 15. UF Artificial Intelligence and Informatics Research Institute. [Demonstration of the IntelliGator classification pipeline, including the Llama 3.3 70B Instruct classifier, the four-tier rubric, the multi-agent architecture, the rubric tuning process, and validation F1 scores for several research areas. Source for the methodology described in Section IV and Appendix A.]

Federal Statistical Sources

National Center for Science and Engineering Statistics. 2025. "Higher Education Research and Development: Fiscal Year 2024. NSF 26-304." Alexandria, VA: US National Science Foundation. https://ncses.nsf.gov/surveys/higher-education-research-development/2024.
National Center for Science and Engineering Statistics. 2025. "Higher Education Research and Development Survey: Survey Description. NCSES 26-003." Alexandria, VA: US National Science Foundation. https://ncses.nsf.gov/surveys/higher-education-research-development.
National Center for Science and Engineering Statistics. 2026. "National Patterns of R&D Resources: 2023–24 Data Update. NSF 26-313." Alexandria, VA: US National Science Foundation. https://ncses.nsf.gov/data-collections/national-patterns/2023-2024.
National Science Board. 2026. "Science and Engineering Indicators 2026: The State of US Science and Engineering. NSB-SEP-2026-1." Alexandria, VA: National Science Foundation. https://ncses.nsf.gov/indicators.

Federal Budget and Policy Reporting

Networking and Information Technology Research and Development (NITRD) Program. "Artificial Intelligence R&D Investments, Fiscal Year 2019–Fiscal Year 2025." Accessed June 2026. https://www.nitrd

.gov/ai-rd-investments/. [Underlying figures from the NITRD and National Artificial Intelligence Initiative Office supplements to the US President's FY2022 and FY2025 budgets. Reported amounts are nondefense budget authority, not awards received; agency coverage and crosscut definitions evolved across reporting years. The series is cited as context for the national AI funding environment and is not directly comparable to UF's sponsored-award data.]

Other Public Sources

University of Florida. 2022–2026. "News Archive." Artificial Intelligence at UF. https://ai.ufl.edu/news-archive. Accessed May 20, 2026. [Continuous archive of UF AI initiative news covering institutional milestones, faculty announcements, research updates, and external recognition. Source for the institutional milestones referenced in Exhibit 1 and the contextual claims throughout, including the May 2023 NSF $20M AI institute award, the November 2023 opening of Malachowsky Hall for Data Science and Information Technology, the founding of AIIRI in November 2024, and UF's 2026 inclusion on the Forbes Public "New Ivies" list.]

University of Florida. 2025. "HiPerGator." Artificial Intelligence at UF. https://ai.ufl.edu/research/hipergator/. Accessed May 20, 2026.

APPENDIX C: EXHIBIT NOTES

The Case at a Glance

This exhibit offers a three-act executive summary of the University of Florida's HiPerGator AI investment and its measured outcomes. **Act I: The Setup** outlines the pre-2020 CPU-era research portfolio, the $95 million four-party partnership, the January 2021 deployment of HiPerGator AI, and UF's commitment to hire 100 AI faculty. **Act II: The Outcomes** reports the measured results: 4.56× growth in AI-classified awards from FY17 to FY24, performance that exceeds three convergent national benchmarks by 2.5× to 3.2×, $511.8 million in cumulative awards across twenty colleges and affiliated centers, and a three-stage mechanism linking infrastructure to talent to sponsored research outcomes. **Act III: The Reckoning** poses the case's central attribution question: What can a vice president for research credibly claim, given the data, the lag between investment and results, and the parallel national surge in AI funding?

Exhibit 1. Research Value Realization Timeline

This exhibit outlines three phases of UF's AI infrastructure investment, spanning pre-deployment expectations, early signals, and measured outcomes. **Phase 1** captures the $95 million four-party partnership and the initial theory of change: compute capacity plus faculty research capability would strengthen UF's competitiveness for AI-related grants. **Phase 2** highlights early indicators within twenty-four months of deployment, including the Research Software Engineering team, the AI Research Catalyst Fund, GatorTron, and the buildout to 204 AI researchers across seventeen colleges. **Phase 3** reports outcomes through FY2026 YTD, including 4.56× growth in AI-classified awards and UF's rise to #26 in the HERD rankings.

Faculty headcount source: Norton, *AI Research Activity FY2022*, UF Office of the Vice President for Research.

Exhibit 2. Indexed Growth Comparison: UF AI Awards vs. National Benchmarks

This exhibit compares UF's High-confidence AI-classified federal awards with three national benchmarks: UF's total R&D expenditures, national higher-education R&D in Computer and Information Sciences, and total US R&D. All series are indexed to FY2017 and expressed in constant 2017 dollars. From FY2017 to FY2024, UF AI awards grew 4.56×, outpacing the benchmarks by 2.5× to 3.2×.

The convergence of the three comparisons suggests a UF-specific effect rather than a simple artifact of national AI funding growth. The Computer and Information Sciences benchmark is conservative: as AI funding increasingly flows through domain agencies and applied fields, including NIH, the US Department of Agriculture, and DARPA, a computer-science-only comparison likely understates the relevant national funding pool.

See Appendix A for the classification methodology and the broader All-AI series.

Exhibit 3. AI Award Breadth by College

This exhibit shows cumulative AI-classified award dollars at UF from FY2021 through FY2026 YTD, across twenty colleges and affiliated centers. Bars are sorted by dollar volume and color-coded by discipline family. The All-AI portfolio totals $511.8 million across 1,023 awards, including Engineering and Computing ($204.3 million), Health and Medicine ($204.6 million), Agriculture and Life Sciences ($57.9 million), Liberal Arts and Social Sciences ($39.1 million), and other fields.

Engineering and Medicine account for 61 percent of the total, while the remaining 39 percent is distributed among eighteen colleges and centers. This pattern suggests that AI-related research has penetrated well beyond UF's historical computing core. Figures use the All-AI series, which combines High and Medium IntelliGator confidence classifications. See Appendix A for the classification methodology. Four UF administrative units with $4.7 million in additional AI awards are excluded.

Exhibit 4. Exemplar AI Awards at the University of Florida

This exhibit features five awards from the AIIRI-curated IntelliGator High-confidence dataset to illustrate the breadth of UF's AI-related research across colleges, federal sponsors, and application domains. A sixth award, UF's role in the DOE/NNSA Predictive Science Academic Alliance Program, is presented separately because IntelliGator did not classify it as AI-related, despite the project's substantial reliance on AI.

The PSAAP example highlights a known coverage limitation: AI-driven awards may be missed if the award metadata does not explicitly reference AI methods. The $10.15 million PSAAP figure represents the government's share of the five-year cooperative agreement for FY26–FY30; $2.13 million had been received as of May 2026. PSAAP figures are sourced from UF's Division of Sponsored Programs. See Appendix A for the classifier methodology and known coverage limitations.

Exhibit 5. Norton's Claim Spectrum: Three Tiers of Defensible Attribution

This exhibit distinguishes three levels of defensible attribution in Vice President for Research David Norton's assessment of UF's HiPerGator AI investment. **Tier 1** comprises capability claims he will defend without qualification because the evidence is direct. **Tier 2** comprises outcome claims he will defend with explicit caveats because the national AI funding surge complicates clean attribution. **Tier 3** comprises tempting narratives he will not assert because the evidence does not support them.

Each cell pairs the anticipated value articulated before deployment with Norton's 2026 view, drawn from his April 28, 2026, interview and his June 2026 review of the draft. The framework's transferability is central to the case. Large-scale return-on-investment arguments often collapse capability, growth, and counterfactual claims into a single narrative. This framework separates them, helping institutional leaders distinguish what they can claim, what they can claim cautiously, and what they should avoid claiming altogether.

The **WARRINGTON CASE SERIES** publishes research-based teaching cases grounded in real institutional and managerial contexts, designed to support graduate and executive business education and professional development through structured classroom discussion.

Published in the United States of America

31 30 29 28 27 26 6 5 4 3 2 1

ISBN 979-8-950151-92-7 (pbk)
ISBN 979-8-950151-01-9 (pdf)
ISBN 979-8-950151-45-3 (ebook)
DOI: https://doi.org/10.5744/9798950151927
Case Number WCS-2026-02

Warrington Press
An Imprint of UF Warrington College of Business
and University of Florida Press
PO Box 140239
Gainesville, FL 32614

GPSR EU Authorized Representative: Mare Nostrum Group B.V, Doelen 72,
4831 GR Breda, The Netherlands, gpsr@mare-nostrum.co.uk

www.ingramcontent.com/pod-product-compliance
Lightning Source LLC
LaVergne TN
LVHW010300230926
848675LV00034B/390
* 9 7 9 8 9 5 0 1 5 1 9 2 7 *